HOW TO BE A GREAT MOM
THAT'S WHAT SHE SAID

RON HOLLOWAY

WHAT SHE SAID, WHAT I LEARNED, AND
WHAT I WANT THE WORLD TO KNOW

Printed in the United States of America

www.ronvholloway.com

First Printing, 2015

ISBN-10: 069258773X
ISBN-13: 978-0692587737

Designed by Solothirty Creative Studio
www.solothirty.com

To my angel, my mother
Stephanie Holloway

May this book be the yellow roses you so loved

"A fool thinks himself to be wise, but a wise man knows himself to be a fool."

-William Shakespeare

HOW TO BE A GREAT MOM

THAT'S WHAT SHE SAID

RON HOLLOWAY

WHAT SHE SAID, WHAT I LEARNED, AND
WHAT I WANT THE WORLD TO KNOW

CONTENT

INTRODUCTION

If you're the type of person that loves your mother, and re-members all her infinite wisdom and "sayings," then you've picked up the right story. From the time my mother passed away, I knew I wanted to write this book. God gave me the greatest gift. And like a great gift, I had a burning desire to talk about my mother and share her with you and the world.

In *How to be a Great Mom*, you will discover the benefits, and ways in which the chapters describe a cookbook of memoirs that gives invaluable information on sacrifice, the importance of resilience and faith, and vivid illustrations of cause and effect. The more you read the more you will ap-preciate the process of adolescence to adulthood.

I wrote this story to chronicle that rich dialogue and point in time throughout my childhood of living with my "Great Mom," the single-woman head of my household – my mother, Stephanie Holloway. The essays are tales of the wisdom, choices, consequences, and confrontation within the aspects of my child-development and parenting skills – aspects that we can all ask of ourselves: What is parent-ing really? Should a parent hover over their kids? Should a parent be the authoritarian? Should a parent be a friend? Should a parent try to be a combination of things? Maybe they should just be an advisor?

Over the course of these chapters you will see someone that was a penny wise and a pound foolish. Over the course of these chapters you will see how each proverb she pro-vided me with was like a slow budding flower. Every day one of her many proverbs provided me new and insightful meaning. Every day one of her many proverbs would influence my character. Every day one of her many proverbs provided me the uncanny ability to be able to critically think. Every day one of her many proverbs would be the thermometer for which many major and minor decisions were made. Her wisdom allowed me to remain consistent in rapidly changing environments.

Before my mother had a severe stroke that paralyzed her and left her in a vegetative state she said, "I raised the man that I always wanted to marry." As a teenager her comments were as clear as mud. But now, one thing is clear: few women could have raised me as well as she did, with all the bad influences and poor examples of role models that surrounded us.

Now you will receive values from my mother more precious than a priceless gem. I pray you will enjoy learning how she balanced parenting like one learns to balance an egg. I pray you will enjoy the reasons why I never listened to my mother – until I did.

1

"WHEN YOU TURN 18, YOU GOT TO GO."

"If you talk to a man in a language he understands, that goes to his head. If you talk to him in his language, that goes to his heart." – Nelson Mandela

What is now affectionately known – or not – as "guerrilla parenting," has a patient zero – my mom. She spread her pathogens, and with my meager mental and emotional antibodies, I could not stomach the "guerrilla style, tough love, get out on your own, and make something of yourself" philosophy my mother drilled into my head day in and day out. My mom was a firm and staunch believer in worth, accountability and a "pick yourself up by the boot strap" mentality.

She was tough as nails and if you were family you had better follow suit. As her only son, I'll give my mom major credit for raising a boy into a man had to be – in and of itself – a herculean task, especially raising a boy with all the negative influences and social ills of my neighborhood. The influences of drugs, hyper-sexuality, gangs and violence inasmuch infiltrated me emotionally and affected my life drastically.

Both my mom and I were hit the hardest by the reality of these influences when I was a teen. Mark was my childhood best friend; he was my ace and my mother's "second son." Mark would show my mother his report card before he showed his own parents. But trouble did ensue. During our high school years, Mark was caught with ounces of cocaine and was incarcerated for drug trafficking; although, the dope was not his, he was allegedly a stash boy for a drug dealer in my neighborhood who had multiple convictions. Rather than tell the truth or "rat," Mark took the charge – essentially ruining his own life. And, the dealer that Mark allegedly held the dope for was the father of his sister's kids.

Was Mark special? Of course. Mark was as articulate as me; he was bright and athletic. Mark could have been Mark Zuckerberg or LeBron James. My mother broke down in tears when Mark was charged and imprisoned. More paradoxical was that I was off to college to play basketball and seek higher learning, while Mark was off to prison learning how to make a dinner meal from a mixture of Cheetos, Doritos, Ramen noodles and summer sausage; he called it a "big boy." Mark was extremely excited to make this for me when he came home.

Still, many years have passed. Last I heard Mark was a bouncer at a nightclub – I guess you can call Mark's situation a paradox. But I still love Mark as my mother did. She always told Mark how much she loved him and how smart he was. And, even with all that – my mother cried these tears a hundred times, not just for Mark, but for all the boys she saw become a victim of habit and circumstance.

Events, stories and tales such as these ended up causing friction between my mom and me. We fought. But only because my Great Mother tried to "lay down the law" and prevent me from suffering from the same afflictions as Mark had. When I turned 18, unlike the circumstances facing Mark, she wanted me to appreciate accountability and responsibility; to her this meant I would be on an even scale in terms of opportunity in society.

Hence, mom never thought it was too early for me to become a man. Concerning manhood, age 18 was simply an arbitrary number to my mother. I remember her saying, "The mother Panda leaves her cub at 18 months – young man you're lucky!" Although I hated many of her lessons, I was lucky. I knew in my heart that she was not trying to get rid of me, or "kick me to the curb." Mom just did not believe at age 18 you just magically became a man; at any age you can be a man.

My mom preached that there is no magic bullet for self-reliability and independence. In her mind it took virtue, character and experience. I hated cutting the grass. I had painting the garage. I hated cleaning my room. When she saw my discontent My mother said, "Son, when you become a man, you will see men that can't even wipe their own noses. Do you want to know why? Because they never did anything for themselves growing up."

I see her truths every day. You've seen them as well? Of course you have. It's the 12 year-old kids in the mall getting pushed in a stroller by their mom or dad. It's the kids that had parents who always cleaned their rooms and washed all their clothes. Or it's the kids that call their parents by their first names and usually show their parents and elders very little respect. Do you honestly see no long-term consequences from such actions?

I have a mental image right now; I can see the smoke billowing out of my mom's ears. She'd blow a gasket if either my sister or I raised our kids that way. I give it to my Great Mother; she totally understood the multiplier effect with regard to parenting. And just as a juxtaposition, she, too, understood the downfalls of what we now know today as "helicopter parenting" — parents that are always hovering around their kids. I've heard stories of "helicopter parents" actually sitting in on job interviews with their children who have just recently graduated college. In my opinion, my mother was right. Great Mom said, "Parenting is like balancing an egg, but hopefully you're more right than wrong." Stories like those above leave men and women unequipped to deal with the harsh realities of life. Sad, but true, everyone does not get a trophy. My mother believed trophy equality led to entitlement. She would have no such thing in our household.

Mom said, "You'll thank me when you're older because my choice to kick you out will help your choices later in life. I'm not here to be your friend, I'm here to be your parent," she would say. And at 18 I left, never to return to the nest. Honestly, I do not blame her one bit because she was right – all's well that ends well, I guess. Hell, Frank Sinatra's father did the same to him. I'm sure Ol' Blue Eyes learned what I had learned along the same process. I learned self-reliance, responsibility and accountability.

Her love and decision to mold me towards independence has immensely benefited my family, my finances and my educational decisions. What a remarkable woman. What a remarkable Great Mom tactic. If my mother were still alive, I would write her endless thank – you notes. But I'd be singing, "I Did it My Way," while I wrote them.

2

"IF YOU MAKE $50,000, LIVE LIKE YOU'RE ONLY MAKING $40,000; THAT'S HOW YOU SAVE MONEY."

"Beware of little expenses. A small leak will sink a ship." – Benjamin Franklin

My sister, my mom and I were in the mall one day. I was maybe 10 or 12 years old. At that age, I was really into baseball. I had all the top trading cards. I loved baseball so much that my mother allowed me to get Sports Illustrated for Kids because I did extra chores around the house. Overtime I filled a section of my closet with old editions of the magazine.

As the story goes, in the mall, there was a Ken Griffey Jr. jersey. I had a really cool poster of Ken Griffey Jr. hitting a home run with the Seattle Mariners in my room. Ken Griffey Jr. had an amazing, some would say textbook swing. But, of course, Mom wouldn't let me get the jersey! Mom said, "Son, we cannot afford it." I didn't want to hear that. I thought, I make sacrifices all the time, and the one time I really want something all you say is "no."

Kicking and screaming, I sat red in the face with that thought circling on a loop in my head. If she knew what I was thinking and what I was calling her under my breath, I would have surely caught hell. Dial soap would have been my dinner of choice – and I use the word "choice" sarcastically. Soap in the mouth was not an unusual consequence growing up as a kid.

Yet, she gave me my space primarily – I believe – because she understood my passion for sports. Still, I threw a tantrum, pouted, and then went mute. She could have easily made me straighten up and act accordingly. All it took was that one Great Mom look or 1,000-yard stare that mothers give their kids when it's time for the foolishness to stop. You know the look I'm talking about. But she didn't. Instead, she subconsciously knew the right discipline and temperament for these kind of circumstances.

We left the mall, and once we got in the car my mother said, "Ronnie, what's the difference between a man working at McDonald's making $40,000 a year but spending $40,000 a year, and a doctor making $100,000 a year and spending $100,000 a year?" I said, "Nothing?" She said, "Exactly. Nothing!" Though pissed at the time, I cannot help but laugh now at her keen "Ms. Master of the Obvious" tactics.

The original great parent, Mom was old school. As an aftershock from the Great Depression, her mother hid money in books; gave pennies as a gift for special engagements; and would call anyone a bastard that couldn't get her what she wanted at the price point she demanded. I felt my grandmother's wrath occasionally because she would order me to scurry to the corner store to buy her cigarettes. In case you were wondering, yes – a child could go to the store and buy smokes for adults back then...my how times have changed?

Still, maybe a product of her environment, and somewhat cynical, my mother believed the capitalistic system was rigged against the average Joe. "Boy, they give you just enough rope..." she'd say. Mom harked that one way to beat the system, or stay afloat in the rat race, meant you had to live below your means. From there, we learned to psychologically treat ourselves as much poorer than we already actually were just to get by. For example, we used recycled clothes, shopped at food banks and used the stove to heat the house.

We actually were food in-secure at times, too. Food in-security means, for example, that white crackers, yellow mustard and sardines was the family table dinner many nights, especially if mom wasn't working. As a side note, in 2013, almost half of US citizens lived in food in-secure households. I remember eating bread with syrup, sugar with water and lemon juice, and canned preserve pears from the food shelters for a desert treat. I was emotionally angry and embarrassed. I would call her all types of names in my head on nights I couldn't have a three-course meal. Yet, as the family provider, these practices worked for my mother.

With what little money we had, these practices of living at or under our means allowed my mother to put money away for dire emergencies. For example, one time the furnace broke down in the middle of winter in Milwaukee. Trust me, cold is not sufficient enough of a word. The house was close to unbearable, which for the time being also ended up with us using the stove to warm the house. No matter, her financial fortitude allowed the family to survive those types of situations and stretch beyond wildest comprehension even now.

I will say, 20 years later, I did see the effects of people who did not make a dollar stretch. I witnessed them very vividly during the 2008 Great Recession. Clear as a car's windshield after a carwash, I remember many of the factors that contributed and were at the heart of the financial crisis. In many cases, people lived well above their means, lacked personal responsibility and took risks by over-leveraging themselves. This didn't happen just locally, regionally or nationally. No. The whole world drank the Kool-Aid; it was like free crack in a drug rehab clinic.

As a result, people now appear smarter about their financial matters. The percentage of home debt abated and overall household savings increased across the board. Funny, I hated my mother's preachy tone, getting picked on by kids, tears, frugalness and material regret at the time, but many people are learning now what my mother had always taught me.

Her analogy didn't make much sense then, but it definitely does now. In her own made-up world, my mother swears she was a financial manager or the poor man's CNBC Squawk Box. I got über tired of hearing her recite, "if you make $50,000, live like you only make $40,000," and so forth. It truly was her fundamental golden budgetary rule. In her mind if I followed that rule my personal finances would remain as sound as the FDIC. My mom taught me well; things I never learned in school. Therefore, I cannot thank my mom enough. I would hardly call her Nostradamus, but I can say her words saved me from much of the heartburn and financial tragedy many others face, have faced and will face.

Through her infinite wisdom, which I often digested as "crack-pot," I honestly know now that it is not what you make, but what you do with what you make. Over the course of many Wisconsin winters, mom taught me financial resilience, budgeting, and how to make a dollar stretch and a nickel scream.

3

"GET YOUR EDUCATION. THEY CAN NEVER TAKE THAT AWAY FROM YOU."

Aristotle said, "The roots of education are bitter, but the fruit is sweet."

This quote would run through my mind as I walked the stage graduating college Summa Cum Laude, I prayed to my mother that day, "Thank you so much, Ma! They can't take it away from me now." Because as a youth, I remember walking to the bus stop passing crackheads passed out on the sidewalk and seeing used syringes and drug packets scattered about.

See my mom believed the lack of education plagued Black society and individuals in general. My mother did not have an enormous amount of higher education, that's not to say she wasn't a wise woman. I mean, c'mon, I would not have wrote this book otherwise.

But my conflicts with my mother and my own personal internal struggles with education began early on in life. I remember thinking maybe life doesn't love me. Early on I had no hope. I couldn't see a way out. I couldn't comprehensively see nor appreciate how education was a way out the "hood," poverty and violence. Education inasmuch was some foreign concept called delayed gratification; something I clearly did not understand nor care about as a young man. Picture the anger within that little person. My logic was simple: who cares about delayed gratification? Who cares about "the ends justifying the means?" "I need to eat right now." Because it's hard to learn a Venn diagram when your stomach is rumbling from hunger. "I need clothes and shoes right now." Because it's hard focusing on anything if you are freezing your butt off while you walk to the bus stop. And this form of logic as an adolescent almost cause me to severely fail a grade in grammar school; I was essentially labeled stupid by school administrators. But my mother fought back hard; I guess my mother knew better and different. Subsequently, mom took me to a child psychologist at Marquette University and in turned out I wasn't stupid at all, but I was actually quite "gifted." My mother smiled when she showed those school administrators the report. Had it not been for my mother's fight with school administrators my landscape may have been much different today. To that end, it was imperative I was explained the importance of education to me in terms of delayed gratification; early on it was hard finding a picture to trace.

And, yet – though my mother had a meager higher formal education, she completely understood the importance of education and all the "doors it opened." But first you had to start with small doors. Or, as she would say, "Big things have small beginnings in this world. Everybody has to start somewhere." Therefore, anytime throughout my life the moment my grades meandered from As and Bs to Cs and Ds, she would get involved. She knew always knew the proper motivations to keep me focused. In terms of correcting my behavior, she sometimes had the tenacity and killer instinct of Kobe Bryant or Michael Jordan chasing championships.

But I can honestly remember thinking how mom was not overbearing or unreasonable. If I did not produce, I would lose privileges. If I disrespected a teacher, I got punished. If I did not get a majority of "good grades" on my report card, I was not allowed to play basketball, which was figuratively a dagger fused and then twisted in my heart. My mom knew I shared a "puppy love" with basketball.

Then as I got older the examination did not recede, nor did her forms of consequences; she just got more clever in doling them out. For example, I underperformed on a grade report in high school, so she did not let me use her car to attend an AAU basketball practice two cities away. The next time I failed at something school related, it wasn't practice that I missed, it was a game. Not only was she showing me that had I let her down with my scholastic performance, but I also let myself, coach and team down as well in the process. Clearly, this was all done in an attempt to show me that life is about choices and consequences, cause and effect, which indeed left my brain branded.

My mother mentally trained me for the marathon, not the race. I grew tired of school because of the relentless focus she wanted me to have. I would mentally vomit and spew hateful words towards her tenacity. But her tenacity was a means for me receiving real self-actualization in the end. At the time, I did not fully appreciate that my mother worked two or three jobs just to allow me to attend a private high school and put provide food on the table. I didn't appreciate that her love had no bounds. Her everything meant me going to college.

Now older, and in hindsight, could I let her down? I knew that I couldn't. It was not until I was much older that I could better internalize her message. I learned powerful lessons. Hard work bred good grades. More knowledge meant enlightenment. The education of enlightenment truly changed my conversation.

As the years went by and I grew into my own man, I began to see the doors opening up that she spoke about, which represent endless opportunities. My Great Mom spoke from a place within her soul dripping with her own blood, sweat and tears. I channeled her spirit. I saw the penumbras of education. I saw the endless possibilities. Mom talked about knowledge as power and education as the "great equalizer" every day. Now I see it for myself. I went to college, studied strong and studied long. I blew away tests. I wrote my papers well. When I would get those papers back with outstanding scores, I would look at the tattoo of my mother on my arm – eyes swollen and filled with tears – and cry.

This is why I graduated college summa cum laude. This is why I prayed to her and said, "Thank you so much, Ma! They can't take it away from me now." With clear vision I could see "the roots of education are bitter, but the fruit is sweet."

4

"CLASS: YOU KNOW IT WHEN YOU SEE IT. AND IT'S NOT FOR SALE."

"A girl should be two things: classy and fabulous." – Coco Chanel

If you ever met my mother you would've never known that she cleaned bathrooms and floors at Marquette University, or worked in a factory-style atmosphere for a living most of her life. You would've never known that she was orphaned and abused. You would've never known that she had to do things for money that she regretted, which she would only tell me when I was older. Why? Because she was the classiest woman I have ever known.

My mother had the type of quiet charisma that could cause a room to become quiet. I noticed this as a kid. I would immediately look up at her to check if she was making faces or doing obscene gestures to cause everyone to stop, stare and become mute. Therefore, I quite often sat courtside with popcorn, a Coke and a smile and watched as my mother seamlessly moved in and out of sophisticated and unsophisticated crowds. She could speak eloquently with my high school principal at length, or speak "hood politics" to the gangsters in my neighborhood.

My mother moved with style and grace like Pam Grier in Foxy Brown; she could court and dress with the best of them – white, black or other. I remember being very proud that she was my mom, except when she would occasionally try to kiss me in public. Really? Yuck! I have always been PDA-lite. That's public display of affection lite – easy on the affection and hold the touchy feely. Still, the lady's persona was every representation of what I wanted and needed her to be.

I assumed that I would never match her panache. Obviously mom did not have a cookbook of class to pass down; she could not tell me to slow-roast "class" at 350 degrees until it's just right. No. My mother could only pass attributes and choice words. For example, she'd say, "having class is not synonymous with wealth or status." Then I'd ask her, "So, how then?" She would retort, "Well, you know it when you see it, boy." And her lesson and theoretical underpinning would continue.

To my mother it meant not being racist, judgmental or gossipy. It meant holding doors for people. It meant showing genuine appreciation when people provide you with a service. It meant deflecting praise and staying humble. It meant presenting oneself well, including, but not limited to clean teeth, neat hair, and clean clothes that fit properly. But, you just couldn't do these things alone, there had to be a nuance, a nuance which made for extremely special people – a cache perhaps. People that others always want around and wanted to be like; it's basically the same obsession with movie stars, like [include a celebrity that you admire].

I desperately wanted to be that guy. Frustrated, for me, class did not appear to be a low hanging fruit. And, even if class was a low hanging fruit, I probably would have suffered from being classy too early in life. Why? For a boy, or young man, class would have come across as "soft" in my neighborhood. I grew up rough and tough; I hate to say it, but where I lived you were either predator or prey. If you couldn't stand up for yourself physically and mentally, you became a target. The same phenomenon holds true in prison as it does confrontations with a schoolyard bully. I didn't want to be that way. I felt schizophrenic. My environment "was what it was." I wanted to do right, but the odds were against me.

Amongst the forest for the trees, I still followed my mother's aforementioned advice, style guide and blueprint. I knew that I had been in good hands. As I got older I became a better person, leader, coach and husband. I learned to finesse the mannerisms and etiquette that I learned from my mother. Coworkers would say, "Your mom must have raised you right. You are such a gentleman." Which, if my mother were still alive, that would have been the ultimate compliment. She would smile ear-to-ear when people said that to me as a kid.

More importantly, though, when I cease to exist , those coworkers will remember the class much more than any possession, job accomplishment or award of mine, similar to how I remember the vivid details of my mother's character. Thank you, Mom! If God had a stylist and life-coach, it would have been you; although, he would have to have a lot of patience and really thick skin.

Great Mom was astonishingly right to tell me that class was

priceless and that it is not for sale. I wouldn't give it up for all the money in the world.

5

"TAKE YOUR VITAMINS AND DRINK THAT COD LIVER OIL."

"It is health that is real wealth and not pieces of gold and silver." – Mahatma Gandhi

Los Angeles Lakers great Earvin "Magic" Johnson was one of my favorite basketball players as a kid. I really wanted to be able to pass the ball like Magic, but I often wondered did Magic's mother peddle supplements to him as a kid?

Why was I so curious? Because my mother was obsessed – I mean she was absolutely obsessed – with giving me vitamins as a kid. My typical early morning routine involved eating oatmeal or cream of wheat, because it apparently "sticks to the bones," and then as sure as the sun goes up and down, I would find a smorgasbord of vitamins perfectly aligned on the counter. Only as someone with OCD could, my mother would have vitamins A, B, C and D aligned with this little brown incandescent bottle of cod liver oil in alphabetical order. The bottle of cod liver oil stood between the C and D vitamin. Therefore, I had absolutely no trouble with the alphabet as a kid. And, still now, I throw up in my mouth a little just thinking about the memory of that brown bottle.

I would hide the bottle or pour some out until it was near empty. Another bottle would appear miraculously like a magic trick – voilà! The pills, though, would get cuffed under my tongue. Like an orderly, soon Mom started to check whether or not I actually swallowed the pills. Both my sister and I would scowl, sigh, beg and plead, but no matter what we still inevitably took our vitamins. Resistance was futile. Remarkably now, as I reminisce, my mother's drug peddling was the best thing for me because I very seldom got sick. I would also receive weird observations from my teachers like, "kid, you have such great skin." Given her modus operandi, I didn't appreciate or understand that Mom just wanted to raise a healthy and strong kid. I didn't understand why she would wipe my chest and forehead down with rubbing alcohol when I had the flu. I know now that she did this because apparently it brings your temperature down. You may laugh, but it worked; the process felt like a cool breeze.

I didn't appreciate nearly eating Vicks VapoRub to "sweat the flu out." I didn't appreciate her vigor for a dehumidifier. I thought all these rituals were senseless when I got sick. Why couldn't I just go to the doctor like the rest of the kids? But here was my real ignorance: I didn't appreciate or understand that we didn't have money for basic doctor visits, so she did the best she could with what she had. I will not say her methods were always right. But, as in the animal kingdom, the mother will do whatever to protect her kin. As animals, or mammals for that matter, in adolescence, we move and stray around aimlessly unconvinced of the world, as I did. Do you know what's it's like to have someone do anything to see you healthy and safe? I had no clue, nor did I care. My mother was only trying to protect me. She was totally right. I was totally wrong. I could not see her intentions clearly at the time.

I have continued some of the much-hated practices from my youth, and I receive those same weird observations and health benefits. People may think I was conditioned by my mother, but it was all for the greater good. I still hear her voice in my sub-conscious saying, "Take your cod liver oil, Ronnie." But I don't. Sorry, Ma. Buck stops there. I do, however, heed the voice by taking vitamins two to three times a week, which I know has my mother looking down with her gorgeous, Hollywood smile.

I have grown to the point now that I joke about these past tales. To this day, I share with family, friends and even strangers my adventures with the damn brown bottle of cod liver oil. I vividly remember burping the oil up back into my mouth sporadically. I can only describe the re-taste as what I imagine the taste of licking carpet and tire rubber would be like. It was often worse than the initial swallow. That phenomenon happened all the time with cod liver oil as a kid; it sucked. I could take cod liver oil at six in the morning, and at 11 it would regurgitate – super random and clandestine-like. If you have ever taken the liquid form you know exactly what I am talking about.

As funny as that wasn't then, it brings some great comic relief to my friends and family now. Laughter is often the best medicine. You may have heard "a teaspoon of sugar helps the medicine go down." Well, I never got a teaspoon of sugar with my meds as a kid. But that didn't mean I didn't receive a big tablespoon of love.

6

"YOU DON'T WANT TO BE BROKE WHEN YOU'RE 30."

"Yeah I hear ya mom. Yeah, yeah, I don't wan' be broke when I'm 31." – Kayne West

Any gamblers out there? I'm not sure what your parents had for the "over/under" for your life expectancy, but 30 must have been my life expectancy according to my mom because I heard this phrase from her quite often. Age 10 was the new 20. She drove me so crazy that at 10, I started doing push-ups like I was getting ready to hit the prison yard. Orange was indeed the new black.

Honestly, I could not blame her; the life expectancy of a young black male at the time – and probably still – was roughly 25. The environmental factors I grew up around caused my mother great angst; she was very fearful that I would become a failure, lack ambition and amount to what she deemed as "walking excrement." My mom would point out people in our circles whose lives were ruined by age 30. Therefore, Mom feared I would not stay focused, which she firmly believed it took to become a success. By 30, my mother had a high school education, filed for bankruptcy, and had been divorced with three children, one of which had cerebral palsy. As harsh and "hand salute" as she could be at times, my mother just really wanted me to achieve more than she had in life. My mom believed strongly in the importance of having a strong foundation. Her words and actions pertaining to the matter did not lack tenacity.

From an early age my mother stressed the importance of maintaining stability and possession in life, in order to withstand life's ebb and flow. Mom took the "by any means necessary" approach.

I learned early about maximizing my resources. For example, my friends would buy a pair of shoes for one large price, but I would a pair of sneakers for a lesser price, keep the change, and put it in my sock drawer. Sometimes I would get two or three pairs for the same price and keep them clean with a toothbrush, therefore ultimately keeping them longer. Or I would do things like sell my toys and games for cash. I remember her telling me that she was proud of me for being resourceful; that fueled me more.

I started working unofficially early. I was learning the importance of work ethic, saving, compounding money, time-management and wants versus needs. I had always done odd jobs, like cleaning a candy store or mopping the floor of a barbershop, but I started officially working around 15. My mom went on a date with the grocery store manager, who got me a job at a big chain; she was always the hustler. And when I got hired she said, "Save your money. You don't want to be 30, looking back and wondering where it [all] went." I could only think one thing: Really, Mom? Really? Because you know I'm only 15, right? Here I am thinking most kids would spend their newfound wealth on clothes, girls and games and here's my mother preaching technology stocks and Roth vs. traditional IRAs.

Yet, now, as a Millennial in my early thirties, I realize everything she said, and everything I did up until this point, was not from a premonition of my mom's fears for her son, but from her tenacity to see her son succeed. I meet individuals every day that were born and raised in amazing households, whom now have major blemishes at my age concerning their "keeping up with the Jones" lifestyle choices, personal finances, and cluelessness concerning retirement. They don't know what they don't know; they haven't received those resourceful chapters from Holloway's Great Mom book. And, although I never really conceptualized my mom's process then, I understand now why she pushed me towards stability, never settling, and investing in myself and not things.

My mom lit an eternal match. I kept hustling. I kept learning. I did less clubbing, partying, and vacationing and I did more volunteer work, which kept me in tune and in touch with society and reality. I kept improving. The whole time I heard my mother in the back of my mind saying, "The most important job in the world is working on yourself, Ronnie – even if they don't give you a dime for doing it." I want to thank my great mother. I learned from her the importance of stability and ambition at an early age. I contribute my successes to mom's Great Mom method handbook, which taught me all that glitters is not gold, and everything that looks good to you, is not necessarily good for you.

7

"VOLUNTEER AND KEEP DIVERSITY AROUND YOU BABY."

"You cannot shake hands with a clenched fist." – Golda Meir

When I was a kid, I was always in a new place, similar to an adventurous coloring book. My mother took us with her as she went to food dispensaries, a lady's home to help her eat, or a cottage for the mentally disabled, as a couple of examples. I remember feeling dragged to these new places, some filled with people, which felt random and out-of-touch. "There was no there, there."

I remember my mother would be in her Rosie the Riveter mode, and so would everyone else; she turned into this little worker bee with extreme focus. But it was very apparent – even to me as a child – none of the people knew each other very well, but they worked in perfect harmony. I could breathe in the collective purpose of good. Yet, I was mad and usually acted out because I hated being there. I usually was the only kid. I was hot under my hood; selfish because I would rather be somewhere else playing basketball or catching bugs and watching them fight – now that was excitement! However, be it heaven or hell, rain or shine, my mother truly experienced excitement working food shelters, clothing drives, fundraisers and other community events.

I did not share that excitement. None of my friends were there, nor did they want to come the millions of times I tried to coerce them to come like, "Dude it will be fun." And I hated the times when she would see a homeless person and ask them, "What do you want to eat?" Next, still dragging me along, she would go and purchase the very meal the indigent person had requested. I know, crazy, right? After dropping the meal off she would say, "Ronnie, it's always better to give food rather than money because you don't know what they'll do with the money." But in those people she saw her own moral dilemma. I believe she saw a small piece of herself in them.

Mom's inertia notwithstanding, and no surprise to me of course, by age 11 she actually made me get a volunteer job. I guess mom figured I had nothing else to do; she was so thoughtful, wasn't she? I worked at Alexian Village of Milwaukee, a retirement home. I hated the job and was terrified at first. The residents were very old. They would defecate on themselves in their chairs and beds, and would shout out horrible things similar to someone suffering from Tourette syndrome.

With time my overreactions abated; it wasn't as bad as the mental torment that I placed on myself. I just feared the unknown. After a while I felt proud like a grown-little man, similar to Kevin Hart. I would play games with the residents, dole out the mail, help with snacks and so forth. After a while, I found the work very fulfilling; it was life changing. I began to see how I was helping and changing lives. I truly and honestly began feeling real joy. And I haven't stopped volunteering since.

Without the effect of false memory or fantasy, I can honestly say that all the volunteer work I did as a kid with my mom, and alone, included remarkable diversity.

And you could not get a more engaging topic than diversity out of my mother. Engaging diversity was tremendously important to her. Sometimes I think she gave a little too much effort towards diversity. At one point, her diversity in boyfriends began to resemble the United Nations – but I digress. Back to the point, my mom started my socialization into diversity early, whereby in my youth she sent me away to school on the south side of town, away from the Black majority. This school was comprised mainly of European, Asian, Latino, Native-American, and a few black kids. I was super angry! I threw a tantrum. I had no security. Where were my neighborhood homeboys? They had stories, rumors, and fun moments from the neighborhood school, and I felt totally left out. I was late on all the hot gossip. I missed the fights. But I had a new fight of my own, which was integrating with this new patchwork quilt or booyah base of kids.

Anxious at first, I began to make friends. In my opinion, kids socialize much easier with one another because they are less defensive and complicated, too slow and ignorant of race and class. Slowly but surely, I began to learn from the diverse group; I learned it was okay to be smart and show my intelligence, whereas in my inner city school I was picked on for being intelligent. I learned their customs, cultures and beliefs. For example, in fifth grade, I learned from my Korean friend the difference between North and South Korea, and the conflict that had ensued. I learned from a Latina friend that I should never call a Mexican a Puerto Rican and vice versa – please don't do it either; it can get sticky fast! All jokes aside, whether they appear trivial or not, I probably would have never learned those things or types of nuances attending my neighborhood school at such a young age. My sense of tribalism had seriously abated.

I did a lot of things that I did not want to engage in as a kid, like volunteering at different places all over and attending schools that I had absolutely no interest in attending. It often came down to an immovable object and unstoppable force. Mom was both. Basically she held the win-win card; it was "Uno out." She and her intentions won early so I could win later in life.

I am winning now because my mom groomed me to be introspective, well-rounded and cultured by engaging me in the vast array of volunteer work, while laying diversity at the forefront. I hated volunteering until I didn't. I hated the new school with all the diversity until I didn't. My mom taught me that both diversity and volunteering are not mutually exclusive. The benefits and beauty of the two intertwined in one another.

Can you see the similarities? Look for them. Thanks to my great mother I learned "you can't shake hands with a closed fist." Thanks to my great mother people walk up to me and say, "Ron, you can talk to anybody." It is because my mother gave me the skeleton key to open the doors, where on the other side of those doors I found people. And my mother told me that, "Remember, people are generally good. We all live in a global village. We all want the same things in life!"

Love. Peace. Happiness. Prosperity. That was the lesson. Glad I learned to keep my hands open. Glad and blessed I didn't miss her class.

8

"YOU'RE WEAK."

"The best way out is always through." – Robert Frost

Close your eyes and pretend for a moment. Imagine that ignoring subtle reverts to consequence. Or, that the inconsequential is consequential. Now imagine each imagination is a childhood reduced to riddles and truths minus the mental cardio, torment-lite (less calories), constant awareness of self and critical thinking. I learned the Freudian ways of my mother. She was the Game of Thrones Cersei of reverse-psychology. And Winter was coming.

How did I manage the mental fortitude? I did day-by-day and year-by-year.

I lived with a woman notorious for reverse psychology. If I were scared of a bully, she would call me names and tell me that I was too weak to stand up for myself which, ultimately, made me stand up for myself and fight back. If I gave up on an instrument too soon, she'd call me weak for giving up saying, "I wasn't strong enough to master it."

When I was scared to swim as a child I received the same psychobabble. Blah. Blah. Blah. One time, very young and before I could swim, she just tossed me in the swimming pool at the local YMCA – sink or swim style. That worked out well for her because I ended my Navy career as a High-

Risk Water Survival Instructor. But the story of my life can be funny like that sometimes. Like Keyser Soze, my mother had a method to her madness.

Her Machiavellian attempts were entirely aimed to increase my self-confidence and mental capacity. She knew that I had the capability to be physically strong, but could my mind match my body? For example, my mom would very rarely attend my basketball games when I was a kid because she was either working, or extremely tired from working and maintaining the household. However, when she did attend a game, her critiques were always aimed at my mental and emotional toughness, or lack thereof, on the court.

Now, I've yet to mention that in the state of Wisconsin, I was a basketball "stand-out" in my youthful days. I was rated a top ten player in the state my sophomore year of high school and at one point nationally ranked. Yet, my mother would criticize me when I showed negative emotion towards a fellow teammate for making a bad play. Or she would tell me to "stop being weak" when I would put my head down after making my own bad play. Examples like these taught me to "man up" and move on to the next play. Or, likewise now, keep pushing forward when times get hard in my life.

My mother once said, "It's hard coming face-to-face with yourself." That all sounds menial in theory. The practice is much more complex, which is why I often – then and now – find myself starring down the barrel of cognitive dissonance. Still, practice makes perfect; it's how I got better in basketball. It's how I got better at navigating life. I have learned from my mother that no mountain is too large. I learned to never be afraid to fly. I learned that my ambition must outweigh my fear. When that happens the sky is truly the limit, as cliché as that sounds.

I learned that my mother wasn't using me as a lab rat. My mother wasn't running trials trying to reject the null. No, her heart was pure. Though arguably unconventional, she wanted to build confidence in me, which she saw lacking in young minority males. Her temperament perfect; she pushed my buttons, ignited my engine and fueled my change. She "spoke to me where I was at," essentially meaning that she built me up when she felt intuitively that I was age-appropriate ready. On its face, "you're weak" was the toughest Great Mom karate chop to my being, but, can you see how she helped me? Reverse-psychology? I can hear my mom whispering, "I told you so."

9

"YOU DON'T HAVE TO HAVE A LOT OF MONEY AS LONG AS YOU HAVE GOOD CREDIT."

"Sometimes poverty is the greatest gift you can ever be given. Sometimes loss is the key that leads you to gain." – Suze Orman

One could assume this is a moronic statement. But my mother knew that if she had no money and no credit, the family's economic placemat would read like a well-known message: No shirt. No shoes. No service.

Please allow me to explain my mother's school of thought: as you may know, credit is the ability of a customer to obtain goods or services before payment, based on the trust that the payment will be made in the future. Therefore, we couldn't outright afford most things we saw on television; however, my mother knew that our ability to have the extraordinary ordinary goods depended entirely on her ability to maintain good credit.

How does a lady cleaning the floors, classrooms and bathrooms at Marquette University afford a $30,000 house in the 80's alone, while raising three kids? She did it through hard work and credit. Mom also wanted us to have decent coats, furniture, school supplies, etc. Can you imagine how good it felt as a kid to walk in school with a Chicago Bulls Starter jacket in the early 90's? Everyone was embracing the Michael Jordan era in Chicago. Mom didn't have a lot of money like Michael Jordan, but she had credit, which allowed me in on the MJ craze, and us to obtain simple goods and services.

Still, Great Mom could be as relentless as an over-ambitious salesperson when trying to get her point across. For example, at age eight or nine, I got my first Nintendo. All I remember my mom saying is, "Boy, you know I'm working two jobs, but I put that thing on layaway." From there, she would explain what layaway was and how it worked. Or, in another instance, she would buy me a pair of basketball shoes that I needed for practice. Yet, she would make me pay a monthly bill for the shoes until the shoes were paid in full; she did this to make me appreciate credit, accountability and responsibility. Sometimes, in an ironic twist, after I paid an item off, mom would hand me back the price of the purchase and make me whole.

When I was younger, I hated her explaining every nuisance of her financial tips and tricks, which might as well have been a foreign language to me then, but she was always teaching. My mother wanted to teach me that the process was the lesson. However, the process can also be the punishment if mishandled or abused. She definitely wanted to make that point ABUNDANTLY clear. I learned credit is the engine to the financial car. And I learned to not burn up the engine. I learned to keep my car healthy and on the road; I take care of "her" and "she" takes care of me. My mother allowed me to sit personal finance shotgun in her car and explained her methodology along the ride – keeping me clear of dead ends.

Mom was a great lady. We never had more than we needed, but what we needed to have we did. She showed me that through hard work, the unobtainable could become obtainable. Though she boiled my blood back then, in her weird way, she taught me money management, financial control and more importantly quid pro quo, Latin for "something for something." As a result this once young fool did not materialize to an old fool. And it is always better to be a young fool than an old fool, I'd say. What do you think?

10

"ALL THESE CLOWNS YOU SEE LINGERING AND SITTING AROUND THE BLOCK NOW, WILL BE DOING THE SAME THING IN 20 OR 30 YEARS."

"Nothing pains some people more than having to think." – Martin Luther King Jr.

This Great Mom lore might hurt me the most. Maybe it is because they say that the "truth hurts." When I return to my old stomping grounds, it inevitably becomes more and more true. I see many of the same people doing the same foolishness as in years past.

There was a time when her foreshadowing had not yet become reality. My mother would push her theory on me saying, "Yeah, that will be you one day." And I would reply, "Yeah, right!" All I saw out of my project window was drugs, crime, prostitution and gang life. In the back of my mind I feared I would actually end up engaged in that cesspool. Never one short on effort, my mother pushed and poked me. My mom and I fought tirelessly. Never physical, except for the occasionally slap if I got "too big for my britches." I would close my door. I would leave the house for days. I ran with the gangs and stayed with older women.

Anything to get me away from what was right.

I was tired of hearing her talk about my friends and the guys that I looked up to. She would say, "They're worthless and don't want anything in life." Although, I knew in her heart of hearts it bothered her to see people not fight for themselves and wallow with hopelessness. Yet, she couldn't help but malign me with them. "You see him and her; they'll be here forever doing nothing," she said. Somehow that anger was directed towards me. It bothered her that they would rather sell drugs than use that agency to get an education. It bothered her that the gang members cared more about "looking tough" than résumé writing or building the community. It bothered her that some women reduced their worth to shoes and handbags.

She would pull me close to her and tell me, "Son, I love you. Please never settle and become content with this environment. Don't drop anchor!" My mother never, ever wanted me to label myself a victim. That is because her imagination was large. She would tell me that there is much to see in this world, and more than just this simple block.

My mother was huge on experiences. Her belief was that the more experiences a person had the more worldly and cultured they would be. Her proof is usually evident when I speak with bigoted, bitter "small-minded" or "close-minded" people. I sense their lack of culture and emotional intelligence immediately. I remember Hillary Clinton referring to "life experiences" as one of the most important characteristics a person should have – reinforcing my mother's own conventional wisdom.

Therefore, I heeded my mother's long-time advice. After

leaving the neighborhood, I had a brief stint playing basketball away in college, shoveled horse manure at state fairs and enlisted in the US Navy. Not only did I travel the world, I filled my young life with a smorgasbord of experiences of which contained different people, foods and culture.

I saw the architecture and economic inequality of Bahrain, the natural beauty and peacefulness of Seychelles, and the castles, romance, food and wine of Spain. In Spain, I remember an old restaurant villa near the river in Rota, where a good friend and I decided to stop and have dinner right after the local siesta. With cheeses hanging from overhead, olive oils abound, and pots and pans available in close sight, the restaurant appeared to be a scene right out of the movie Casablanca.

As we sat down the shop owner, of his own accord, continuously shepherded in to my friend and I various different small plates, or tapas. Each plate was a new experience of flavor, texture and culture. With the white noise of the river in the background, I could gleam from the owner his eagerness for us to experience the delicacies of his culture. Moreover, he was excited for us to taste things that he was sure we had never experienced in our native land.

And with the food, he also provided the history of the small Mediterranean town and life lessons to two impressionable sailors while we sipped vino. Back in the old neighborhood, my friends, family and the people that I grew up around could not relate when I told such tales. Experiences like that of the restaurateur in Spain had opened up my eyes to the world.

So there I was, at home, and feeling like I was speaking with people from another land. I didn't see them as cool anymore, just ignorant. Their paradigms remained the same; they were stuck in a proverbial time shaft or wormhole, whereas I had a complete paradigm shift. I could see in their eyes, too, that my stories offended them. I had done much and been to many places. It changed me. Without these experiences would I have remained similarly ignorant?

What wisdom my mother had. Her foresight now, nearly empirically testable as I watch those people 20 years later living the same life now as they were then — unwilling to change, unwilling to grow, unwilling to learn, unwilling to explore new sights and new visions. I hated with a fury that my mother would lump me in with them as an adolescent. But her charade was a lesson nonetheless: Become the ills of your environment or adapt and overcome; it still rings true 30 years later.

PANTHEON OF MOMS?!

In my opinion, neither I nor anyone else can say one parent-ing style is better than the other. I am not in the business of exclusion, drama, or conflict; although, I would definitely sell a lot more books if I were. I'm sure one can be suc-cessful with one of the parenting methods I mention in the pantheon, or a combination of a few – different strokes for different folks.

They say for a great match in boxing, "styles make fights." Likewise, different mommy-ing styles complement other mommy-ing styles, which results in a Great Mom. The fol-lowing are some of the most commonly talked about par-enting styles.

FRIEND MOM

FRIEND MOM

I cannot tell you how often I hear parents articulate this insatiable need for friendship with their kids. I guess the need for friendship is innate? Who doesn't like friends? And who wouldn't want more friends? We love when our friends and followers online give us "likes," "thumbs ups," and validation. But what about when that person is your mom?

Friend mom is hip. Friend mom is cool. You can tell friend mom anything; she's like one of the boys or girls. All your friends like your friend mom. But, would you trust one of your friends to raise you? Probably not.

For me, I would've turned out considerably worse if my relationship with my mother was based entirely on friendship, and vice versa. Why? Friends can be enablers. Friends will not always tell you what you need to hear. Friends negotiate. Friends are usually peers, more like Wayne's World and less Billy Blanks. Had my mother acted entirely as a peer or friend, I'd most likely be lazy. Do you think that would have changed my life's motivation a bit?

My mother quite often said, "I'm not your damn friend! I'm your mom." That was enough said, I knew what she meant.

Had my mother treated me as her friend, I could see myself being less respectful of elders, lacking discipline and mis-educated in the importance of the role as a parent. Why respect adults or elders if respect wasn't a big deal to mom? And, honestly, friends don't scold one another; that's why they're friends. Duh.

In my opinion, it's cool to be friendly with a son or daughter; it's okay to respect their positions; it's okay to want to always see them happy. These are all the things friends of your son or daughter will supplement to your parenting. Let their friends be their friends. You be the parent, or Great Mom.

TIGER MOM

TIGER MOM

Were you forced to take 20 hours of piano lessons a week in your youth? Were straight A's a requirement or punishable by death? Yes, there it is – tiger mom. Tiger mom is probably associated with the most controversial parenting style. The tiger mom is relentless and always on the prowl for any competitive edge in their child's success. The tiger mom is very strict with her expectations of excellence. The tiger mom is infatuated with the need to have a child that is "gifted" or extraordinary.

But wait. There's more.

As with most things perceived as flawless, there's a drawback. The tiger mom's overbearing stripes has the potential to graduate a child to a life of social awkwardness and seeing every peer as a competitor (alpha male and alpha females). In my opinion, some of the offspring have a propensity to lack morals because of the overbearing indignation to reach success at all costs. At the height, the offspring may suffer from deep ravines of depression and anger when the chips are down. Have you seen the movie Carrie? Carrie had a tiger mom – no doubt.

With all that said, many tiger cubs have borne extraordinary benefits and remarkable talent, but at what cost? Buyer should definitely beware. Trust me, as an adult I know tiger cubs or, should I say the offspring of tiger moms, instantly. One trait is a lack of bedside manner. And, if you met my mother, you'd know she was tough, but hardly a tiger. I had to get good grades, but getting straight A's wasn't impera-

tive. I didn't have to get a gold star or gold medal every time. I didn't have to believe I was "gifted." I was pushed, but I was mostly loved for being me, and my own uniqueness.

My mother would say, "All things have a saturation point. And when that point is reached, it's ugly." I guess my mom had a few tiger stripes, but God I'm glad she didn't have many.

KNOW-IT-ALL MOM

KNOW-IT-ALL MOM

She probably knows it all. And is sure to remind everyone she's the smartest one in the room (probably in a passive aggressive manner). This might be a result of the repetitive proselytizing regiment. Or it might simply be a personality or some internal complex.

A child under this condition subconsciously looks to mom, and only mom, for advice, reassurance and validation. I'm not saying that's entirely bad, but it can be. So how does that personally affect critical thinking? How does that personally affect a smorgasbord of thought? How does that affect socialization?

An offspring from this parenting type may appear skittish of external advice and philosophy. I personally believe my greatest attribute is my mindedness. I've garnered a buffet of information, elicited from all types of sources and socialization. Through trial, wisdom and experience, I have been able to filter in and out importance, and conventionalism.

As my mother would say, there are things she could not teach me. There were certain things she believed I had to learn on my own, out in the world. I had to learn and experience racial profiling. I had to learn and experience what it means to be a man. I had to learn and experience on my own what it meant to fight for something I truly believe in or care about. I don't believe I would have as great of a Great Mom experience with a know-it-all mom. Why? It is said, "Story telling is told through a certain prism, and everything you are affects the way you tell that story."

GUERRILLA MOM

GUERRILLA MOM

In several chapters of this book, I detailed aspects of my mother's tough love, get out on your own, do it yourself methodology. The guerrilla mom believes strongly in self-reliance; that was Stephanie at heart. My mother never cared vociferously whether or not I became rich or a CEO like tiger mom. My mother only wanted me to have the ability to take care of myself. Mom showed me, and articulated to me, there is "more than one way to skin a cat." And there's more than one way to live life – a happy life. From her, I learned critical thinking and deductive reasoning and resourcefulness.

Why'd she care so much though?

My mom didn't believe everything was a trophy. Life doesn't work that way. And because I realized everything wasn't a trophy early on, I realized trophies are only possible through hard work and resourcefulness. My mom set me up well. I grasped critical life qualities that serve as adrenaline and dopamine on the road to complete independence.

I'm glad she was unconventional with her parenting methods. As with any parenting technique within this pantheon, you must know and understand your child. My mom definitely understood me, including what levers she needed to pull to motivate and prepare me for the future. Most people suggest my mom closely resembles a guerrilla mom. I'd be inclined to agree.

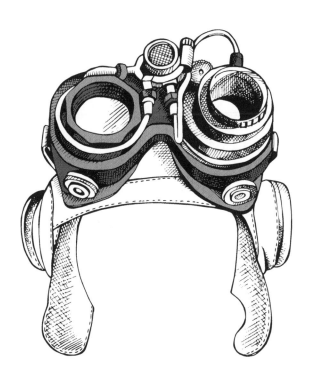

HELICOPTER MOM

HELICOPTER MOM

"Go! Get to the chopper!" said in the iconic Arnold Schwar-
zenegger voice. If you don't know, that's a pop culture line
made famous by the former California Governor and actor
in the movie Predator. The helicopter (or chopper) in the
blockbuster hit movie resembled safety and protection. The
helicopter mom acts as the same in parenting, like a figura-
tive protective shadow (literally in some cases) for their kids.
The helicopter mom will entirely select their child's foods,
friends, activities, and worse, behavior. The helicopter mom
does all this in the guise of their kids' "best interest" and to
keep them "safe and sound."

But really, the helicopter mom actions are a reactive to anxi-
ety, insecurity and over-compensation.

My mother religiously didn't believe in being overly protective in my youth; her style was more like Goldilocks: neither
too hot nor too cold. Mom would say, "I know those types
of parents, and I know their kids. Those kids end up like
an animal out of the cage when they get older and out of
the house." Stephanie took a trusted, but verified approach
with my sister and me. She trusted that we could be responsible. And she would verify we satisfied responsibility. If I
was responsible, that bred trust. Trust bred unilateral decision-making. Unilateral decision-making breeds a seamless
transition to adulthood.

Mom said, "I can't be around you forever. So when there are
no street signs around, how will you know which way to go?"
Thank you mom, for providing me the roadmap to life.

NOTES

_____

_____

_____

_____

_____

_____

_____

_____

_____

_____

_____

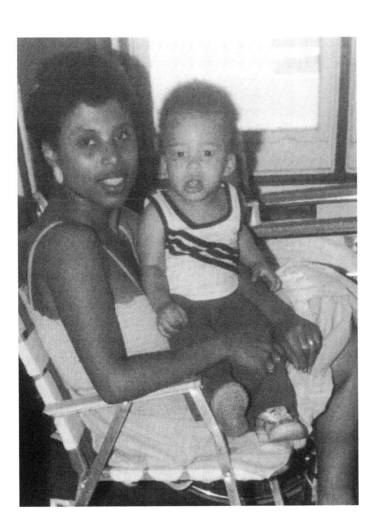

ABOUT THE AUTHOR

Ron Holloway is a Navy Veteran and public speaker, best known for his book: *A Courtesy Flush Goes A Long Way*. Ron grew up in Milwaukee, Wisconsin, traveled all over the world, and now resides in the Washington, D.C. metropolitan area with his wife, an electrical engineer and graphic design artist, and their two French bulldogs.

To continue receiving free tips and updates, sign up for Ron's newsletter at RonVHolloway.com

Two non-profit organizations will receive a portion of all book proceeds for the life of the book: The Brain Aneurysm Foundation and Boys and Girls Club of America.

Made in the USA
Middletown, DE
29 November 2015